GRAFFITI

MUSINGS ON MATTERS "SPIRITUAL"

MAHESH HANGAL

ISBN
Paperback 979-8-89724-967-1
Hardcase 979-8-89777-274-2

Dedicated to

Wayne Liquorman

Teacher of Non-duality

True humility is in realizing
that each of us has been created
with a role to play and that none
of us were consulted beforehand
about what that role was to be
– Wayne Liquorman

A Word...

Whenever I have tried to write, I have always found that the immaculate empty sheet of paper in front of me, expresses, whatever I have to say much more eloquently than any words I might use.

Yet the miracle is that these musings have happened as naturally and as spontaneously as the happening of breath.

Graffiti?

A brief look into astronomy will reveal that this planet of ours is nothing more than a little speck of dust. If we take a minute off and reflect on the sheer magnitude and diversity of the universe we inhabit, we come to the conclusion that musings of any kind, however profound & insightful can at most only be... graffiti on the part of the minuscule human intellect. These musings of course are no exception.

Hence the name 'Graffiti'.

Graffiti... is a collection of "my own" musings culled from my personal diaries which I have been keeping ever since I can remember.

– Mahesh Hangal

P r a i s e F o r ' G r a f f i t i '

I found *Graffiti* enlightening. I whizzed through the book first, then went back to read the meditations a couple per day, to fully absorb the wisdom. There are gems in this book which, when contemplated, apply to the meaning of our daily lives and the reason for our existence. I thoroughly enjoyed the book.

– Bill deMello, Author of 'The Happy Wanderer', biography of

Anthony deMello, and 'Swansong – Anthony deMello's Last Seminar'.

Mahesh Hangal has been blessed with a deep understanding of Advaita. *Graffiti* is awesome, and enjoyable reading. Here is a favourite – "It's basically a one word story: Destiny".

– Jaya Arun Nagarkatti (daughter of the

advaitic sage Ramesh Balsekar), Bangalore

In the multitude of books appearing in print here is a gem that glimmers by its inner glow of heartfelt thoughts that find articulation in soft feather-like words. The words make the reader realize how deep are our true and genuine thoughts and how inadequate is language to voice them. 'Graffiti' leads the reader into quiet contemplation and to the silent world of self realization.

– G. C. Tallur, B.E.B.A. F.I.E. Former Secretary,

Public Works Department, Government of Karnataka

I enjoyed the pithy and powerful aphorisms you have written. That you live in an intuitive and spontaneous way is pretty much evident.

– Nithya Shanti, world-renowned spiritual teacher,

seminar leader, writer and educator, Pune

I am reading your book. It's amazing!

– Sitar Maestro Pt. Purbayan Chatterjee

The book is beautifully done. The utterances are unusually profound and enlightening.

– Dr. Anil Awachat, Writer, Social Activist, Academy Award

Winner, Director (Muktangan De-Addiction Centre), Pune

The 'musings' are in. May I congratulate you on your Wayne fling. I was glad to have laid my hands on your lovely book.

– Librarian, Ramana Ashram Granthalayam, Tiruvannamalai

I have enjoyed every single page of your book which is full of your words of wisdom. I am privileged to know you.

– Dr. Mukesh Gandhi, CEO, Creative Synergies Group

Detroit, USA

The title *'Graffiti'* is a misnomer. The musings herein are no graffiti. I have found insights on these pages that are astounding to say the least.

– Dharmadas Barki, Green Oscar Award Winner

Chairman & Managing Director, Noble Energy Solar Technologies

Ltd., Hyderabad

Mahesh! It's an exquisite, cute looking book. Your thoughts in *Graffiti* are exceptionally refreshing to read.

– K. Chandrashekhar, Author of

'Stopped in Our Tracks - Stories of U. G. Krishnamurti in India'

(Series 1, 2 & 3)

... so excellent. Straight from the heart.

– Clifford W. DeSilva, Director, The Goa Institute of Counselling,

Navelim, Goa

At the most you may understand what it means
to understand, but you will never be able to tell
what is it that you understand!

When you are willing to give EVERYTHING
No one can take away anything from you

For many, the teacher remains only a window
Only for a rare few does he become a door

What's present, cannot say, that it's absent!

At no time did I allow the process of seeking God
distract me from my experience of Godliness

Even when you go against the flow
You go with the flow...

No answers - only mirrors. The wise man simply keeps...
pointing to the fact that life is its own answer

All needn't be well in order for all to be well

I am no fatalist
There are some fires you can't run from!

It is impossible to be cheated...
when you expect nothing in return

Cling to faith? But why?
If one really had faith one would let-go
One wouldn't cling!

The allure of the destination is all but gone
What a wondrous tour guide I have had!

Read the fine print! And you will know…
Life has no responsibility of being fair to you!

The heartrending agony of this drama called life
is that… one is cast into the straightjacket of a…
single role forever and forever. But then, it's only
a drama… it's only a role

Birth is a happening… Death is a happening…
Why should living be any different?

FREEDOM - can it mean anything other than not caring
what happens the next moment?

Clock's Captive… !
You think YOU have time… TIME has you!

The one you are looking for
is busy playing you!

A problem is a problem only if it's MY problem
Now how mean is that?

Fiction is the only reality

The play goes on...
It's we, who leave the theatre

The very first step is to understand
that there is no such thing as ego
It is also the last step

You say YOU decide! Yes... you ARE the decider...
make no mistake... but then, WHO decides the decider?
Therefore, is your decison... truly YOUR decision?

To be is the only evidence! There is no proof of reality
other than being it

The real teaching strikes down the intellect
who is trying to grasp the teaching!

Heaven... can at best...
only be an oasis in hell

'I can't' expresses the human predicament
more ACCURATELY than 'I won't'

What's it that you want?
Has life not already given everything?

Just look!
It takes no effort to see things as they are

Point taken … ! Both ARE illusory
But I would still prefer a happy dream
to a nightmare

The 'purposeful' life ironically misses
the very purpose of life

And once you get infected with a name and form...
You're doomed...(!) it's only gonna be a matter of time

The task is cut out - how to get rid of the ego
How to make something that doesn't exist disappear

You don't have the experience of unity
You ARE the unity

Peace may be a bit dull at times
but it beats all the other alternatives

Mind... is an instrument that personalizes
the impersonal process of living

The teaching of the Sage... is really, the teaching of...
the seeker! Because it's the SEEKER who draws forth
the teaching!

Am I the ocean... ? I don't KNOW... and I don't CARE
That, I am not the wave is more than I can handle!

If you don't meet your destination
at EVERY step of the journey...
It's no path at all!

The turbulence of the river disappears when it meets
the ocean because... its's fundamentally the river that
disappears

I believe in blessings and curses
I only don't know which are which

The incorrigible nonduality-buff that I am
I exist, even if only to prove... that-I-don't!

The path that doesn't die, even after
reaching the destination...
THAT'S the one to look for!

We all have a say!
But it is not for us to decide

I know, but when you ask me I don't

EGO'S MISSION STATEMENT - I don't mind
losing my head as long as my crown is intact!

Every prayer gets answered... may be not in the way
you want it to be

To love the other is to see the face of God
To know that 'there's no other' is to be God Himself!

You will never get the true picture
There simply isn't one!

NOT TWO
The wave is the ocean
The ocean is the wave

It's the other way round... !
You don't have peace because you meditate.
Because you're DESTINED to have peace...
meditation happens. The effect... is the cause... !

For the Sage there is no such thing as morality
so He can never be immoral

Now... a Sage can say and DOES say that He does
not like pain... but He can NEVER say, that pain
SHOULDN'T be there... ! HUGE difference!

I am a religious man
I have a personal religion of my own

It's God... who becomes both the miserable seeker...
and the compassionate Guru, and plays with Himself!

I myself have gone missing
What a BIZARRE journey

I leave no footprints in the sky
The sky itself is my footprint!

It's all here
Hidden in the open
You are what you are looking for!

What to do... ? Do the next thing! It's as good
an answer as any!

I might look like I am doing nothing
But isn't that how whole existence looks?

You are afraid to be ordinary; THAT'S your misery

Plain and simple... !
The realization... that 'I am better off without
myself'... is what, enlightenment is all about!

Death is the end of story
which never started anyway

If you have a clue as to who you are, so be it
Just don't follow the clue

To be a cage-maker, and yet, be candidly
in love with freedom, is to be a free man!

'Truth'... is noise to the person
who understands it

It is the apparent defects of a Sage that really
disguise Him

Double whammy!
There is no one to get "it". Nor there is an "it" to get!

We seek non-existent goals
What's more... we even find them!

You know what! We don't want a thing
but then we don't have a choice!

Whether he knows it or not... all...
that the spiritual seeker is truly seeking
is PEACE and HARMONY... in DAILY LIVING
Samsara and Nirvana are one!

No matter how noble the presence of will
can only exist in defiance of God!

Where is the difference unless you
differentiate?

To understand your side of the story
I should have no story of my own

The journey is all there is...
One is stuck with the mirage!

Call it 'The biology of enlightenment' if you will
Ask yourself just this one question - "Does it operate
in my life?"

The mountain does nothing to change
the course of the river

Just say any damn thing. Nobody wants the Truth
We just want an answer

The song sings you... as much as you sing the song!

STRANGE curse this... !
You have EVERYTHING! But then you want MORE!

You pay God a great compliment
when you ask nothing of Him

You are not the source of the doing, you are merely
the instrument through which doing happens
There is less to you than you think

Freedom isn't the ability to choose
It's quite the opposite!

An illusion is an illusion...
only if I accept it as one!

Except waiting one can do nothing
to ripen the fruit

Sometimes... the best tool for exposing a good lie
is an even better lie!

All understanding is fundamentally
a misunderstanding!

What good will asking "Who am I?" do?
The one who will get the answer is false!

Beware the signpost!
THE PATH IS EVERYWHERE... !

When you overlook the obvious, it's obvious
that it isn't you that's looking

A manufacturing defect, as it were… !
I can only appear to be what I am not!

The idea of liberation is the one
that is creating bondage!

The hope that arises out of hopelessness
THAT'S the one to hope for

Thank God spiritual practices don't help
Because-you-don't-need-them!!

The script life has written for you...
is all the script-ure you will ever need

It's a catch 22 situation!
YOU, want to stop thinking... but
the very basis of thinking, is YOU

Freedom from the burden of *ajnana* ... is awakening
Freedom ... from the burden of *jnana*, is deliverance

When I say you don't do a damn thing
all I mean is, you are not separate ...
from the thing, that's doing all the doing

The realization that meaning is the curse of the mind
must somehow come about
And it's not always an easy realization

Walking on earth is as much a miracle as walking
on water
It's just that one is familiar... the other unfamiliar

Just say the obvious! And you would have said all
that's there to be said

Pleasure... is merely pain in disguise!
One LONG HARD look... and the mask slips

The trick... is to know oneself as the Ocean
but to continue to abide as the wave!

All the renunciation that one really needs
is to stop being what one is not

The dreamer lasts... as long as the dream
Stay put!

Search for it where you have lost it, not where
there is light! Escapism can get so very subtle

So goes a popular Zen saying "Look at the moon
don't bite my finger", but then biting the finger...
may be someone's way of looking at the moon!

You are more than real
You are reality itself!

Even a good thing isn't as good as nothing!

You may not always find peace in meditation
But you will always find meditation in peace!

What is happening... ? When nothing is happening?

Search for Truth... if you must!
But make sure you have lost It!

The ego only ensures its continuity
by seeking an egoless state

Is enlightenment the end of suffering? Yes, and No
There WILL be suffering... but YOU won't suffer!

Whose karma? What karma?
It's only the karma of life!

No 'you'. No 'next'
The path ends where the walker disappears

Happiness cannot be found
because it was never lost

If ALL don't win
... all lose

The Sage cannot help being a Sage
The psychopath cannot help being a psychopath
Hey, this match is fixed!

That... which goes in search of light
is light itself!

What is there can't be wrong, can't be false
because it's there!

The goal of life... is life ITSELF
And it's not always an easy goal to set!

Even after enlightenment thoughts continue to happen
The waves WILL be there
But the ocean is not concerned

Who says 'A name is just a name?'
Without names, we have nothing!

How can you not know what enlightenment is?
It's what you are!!

The final understanding is a state of *bhakti* not knowledge

When you mistake… the concept for the Truth
You're in bondage!

Truth sat, drank tea, and smiled
The real teaching is the teacher himself!

If ALL... take the masks off...
How will the play go on?
NO MASKS... NO PLAY!

The truth of the moment is ITSELF...
the truth of all eternity

If every clue only deepens the mystery
One is on the right path

The question has to go, that's half the job done. And
it's not replaced with an answer, that's the other half!

"The map is not the territory!" asserted the clever
"But without a map there is no territory at all" the
wise were up to it
But not one wondered... "Who does maps?"

The "unselfish" man is only more greedy
For he longs for greater fulfillment...
than the selfish man

Why is the world ruled by appearances?
Because-there-is nothing-behind!!

Desires... do get fulfilled! It's just that
every time they may not be your own

Never ever did the master say one thing
and life another
Spirituality… is life itself!

Timidity becomes a problem only when you want
to be brave
No alchemy like the alchemy of acceptance

To ASCRIBE… causes for life's happenings
is but a myopic way of looking at life!

All we intend to do is to die to the self
to who we are
What we call meditation is but a roundabout
attempt at hara-kiri

Ask yourself...
Are you really happier than your dog?
The answer could well surprise you

The storm that drowned you, carried someone
safely to the shore

There is no in ... ! There is no out ... !
Yet so many busy finding a way out

You say "GOD'S GRACE" when things go your way
And "GOD'S WILL"... when things do not! Clever you!

Every season brings its own joys
... and sorrows!

You are not the dreamer
You are only a dreamed character!

It's a blessing to be born as a seeker
… and a tragedy to die as one

The ego only claims!
That's its full time job

Mine is an everyday story
No wonder no one listens to it!

Being a nobody... enables you to do the thing...
the moment calls for - LIFE BECOMES SIMPLE

I am not saying there is nothing wrong with the world
All I am saying is it can't be any different!

My philosophy of life has been to do what seemed
like a good idea at the time
It has never let me down!

Apart from the story of the world
I have no story of my own

The reason you can't see...
something that's present...
is because, you-are-absent

A story can only stay with you
long after it's over, only if, it has stayed with you
long before it was told

We ask "Why me?" when we break a leg
We don't ask "Why me?"
when we win a jackpot!

Look at the dance... !
Hopefully you will spot the dancer

You CAN be the master of your destiny
Only if you are so destined!

Nobody home!
My life... is an act without an actor

You don't live in the present moment
You ARE the present moment!

Conned by god, so to speak... !
We don't have choice; we only have the illusion
of choice

The river reaches the sea only because
it remains unattached to its banks

The real function of a mirror, is to help see that
there is no one to look into it!

Be dead... ! It's one sure way of reaching
the shore. SINK... then you'll land

There was never a question of wave
becoming the ocean
The wave IS the ocean!

For one who has become desireless...
can there be anything to think or say or do?

THAT'S the final milestone - The death of insight!
... the Sage has no insight whatsoever!
Insight... can only arise from a state of confusion

How can "anyone" know the truth? An illusion
can only know that which exists within its realm!

I sing the same song too... but never
in quite the same way... ! I can't tell you
what the Master EXACTLY said. But I can
always tell you what He EXACTLY meant

Everything that occurs... occurs in the same way
the way your nose occurs on your face

The moment you ask "How to live?"
You have already created a problem

Blah Blah Blah – a wrong teaching is just that
And so is the right one!

The character in a movie does not know
what is going to happen next
But the thing is the character who has realized
he is only a character does not care anymore!

If you have to remember that you are home
it will only be because you are not!

I am EVERYTHING!
But then all I want to be... is to be something

You see… ? There is knowledge that knows
and there is knowledge that-does-not-know
It's the latter... !

Rather than the faith that moves mountains
I would have the one that rests happily
with the way God has placed them

My story... ? Here you go...
It's basically a one word story - Destiny!

A Leela … a divine-play, as it were!
He who talks here is also the one, who listens there!

Got the point... ?
Throw away the pointer!!

No yesterday, no tomorrow, no today…!
In my story… everything-happens-at-once!

If you don't care whether you win or lose
You have already quit the game!

The mirage doesn't disappear as you go near
It just was never there!

My hope for you is not that you become
who you want to become, but that you find peace
with who you are!

You only hoodwink yourself when you say
you have CALLED OFF the seeking!
A seeker... can only CEASE to be a seeker

The universe can do whatever it wants
Period

You trust this, that and what not... !
... not everyone can trust Nothing

Buddha... is only a ghost in the seeker's mind

Sleep happens! Dreams happen! Waking up happens!
Tell me one thing that YOU do

ONLY GOD KNOWS!
Truer words were never spoken

Understand peace you may... but then...
you miss the peace that surpasseth all understanding

Even if you succeed in saying the unsayable
You succeed only to fail!

You like the idea of being on a picnic
No wonder your ego-trip lasts a life time!

You think the Sage knows better
He doesn't know a DAMN thing!

Just see the dream as a dream
Isn't a way out part of the dream too?

It's not that the Sage has all the answers
He just does not have any more questions!

The master reveals the question, not the answer

"It is too plain to see!" assert the wise.
But the thing with such an assertion is...
it is totaly useless to two sorts of people...
those, who can see... and those who cannot

You see? What we call cause and effect relationship
is simply a story we tell!

Lies about Truth
That's what the scriptures are!

If you say, you have reached all by yourself
You probably haven't reached far!

Real affluence means... not wanting anything
from anybody. Not even from God!

My end is my beginning
... all I can do... is wait!

You don't have to go through the dark night of the soul
to be what you are

If you have free will tell me what your
next thought is going to be?

There is nothing wrong with the world, it's just that
you have taken it for your home

For once, why not call it a day
before the day begins!

I am born... I will die...
Yet I am eternal!

You can quit any damn thing… provided
the "damn thing" is ready to quit you!

There is nothing to be done!
… but only if you want Nothing

… running out of questions is AWAKENING
running out of answers… is DELIVERANCE
… doesn't that just say it all?

It's a fine distinction! Thought is not the problem
THINKING is the problem!

Water-bubble like... !
My manifestation is ITSELF the harbinger
of my annihilation

ALL roads lead to Rome
Take any you fancy... !

What prevents you from doing the right thing
is the right thing ITSELF

Happy is the man who is Nothing
But how many of us are that lucky!

If the path is your own
you will soon find... that there is no one
who's walking the path

The goal if any, is to be an ordinary man
without the ordinary man's problems

You would have GRASPED. Had your grasp
not exceeded your reach

What is the Sage trying to tell you...?
He isn't trying to tell you anything! He is only
trying to erase all that the world has told you
and all that you have told yourself!

You do what you do and you get what you get!
Period

Guru! What for?
Do you need light to see light?

A mirage surely gives false hope
But that's all some people need!

Once you ask 'What's the meaning of everything?'
You stop asking the meaning of this and that

GRAFFITI

To go beyond... the seeker has to let go
of the conceptual knowledge, just like...
a pole-vaulter has to let go of the pole...
in order to jump over an obstacle

You can sure win the war
Only don't forget to leave the warrior behind

If ALL craft wings...
Who crafts the sky?

To seek something from life
I have to be separate from it

You will find a place in heaven
Only if you have lived in one before!

If there's one thing that's standing
between you and enlightenment...
it's... "your idea of enlightenment!"

There isn't anything to look for
All you have to do is look!

It's rather strange... ! Only after we 'awaken'
does life begin to appear like a dream

And imagine... one day we would be gone...
Gone forever and forever... What a relief... !

Once the puzzler dissolves into the puzzle
The puzzle falls into place

It was ludicrous! Every signpost... resembled the
destination! There was no way I could arrive!

As long as you believe in believing, it doesn't matter
what you believe in

If you don't know what you're looking for…
how will you recognize it when you find it?

It's only when the character leaves behind the story
that the real story begins!

Asking if God exists, is like…
the painted figure asking if the painter exists

It's the same picture! Only each see it differently

YOU do not get on with life
LIFE gets on with you

The gate is open – you're building keys … !
All spiritual effort is like knocking on an open door

There is nothing... you can do, except
describe the movie

To have the peace of deep sleep...
in the waking state is to be enlightened

The bargain is struck only once!
The Master gave me Nothing... and I took it!

It's like this... you sing a song and the song
is melodious
You're that melody

In fighting with the phantom
You make the phantom real!

Behold! My strange new sanctum! A place like no other
Everything is nothing... ! And nothing is everything here!
Here, nothing is present... and nothing is absent!

You ask the impossible... !
How can a character in a novel ever understand
why the novelist created it?

That's the tragedy... !
Throw the garbage out
And you throw the WORLD out!

Generosity uncalled for… !
Mind sets the fire, then calls itself the fireman

Only because someone is pulling its strings
does the kite appear to be flying freely

Simple imprisonment for some

Rigorous imprisonment for some

Facing life imprisonment, for sure... we all are

"Do I ever meditate? I never stop!!"

The moment you want to know...

you start accumulating ignorance

Why is the ego there? Because without the ego

life as we know it cannot happen

Vairagya... is the absence of involvement
not the presence of dispassion

Pretend that you ARE
And you only postpone yourself

Life is a sport. You fish for sport
not to catch fish!

You can't help but lose
I can't help but win
The human condition can be summed up
in one word - Helplessness!

The interesting thing
about your face...
is you-don't-have-one

No matter where you are pointing
You are always pointing at yourself!

All you can do, is GO through the scripture...
And wait till the SCRIPTURE goes through you

Everything does not happen for a reason.
God just cannot be so unreasonable!

As long as there is one who is happy
There is one who is unhappy

There is no right action or wrong action
There is only action!

REALITY is the screen, LIFE is the movie
Spirituality is the bond between the two!

Do your bit
I did mine
I let the world take care of itself

You needn't be good to feel worthy & complete
You need only be yourself

Nothing is in your control
Yet there is no power outside of you

Even the one who sees everything as a lie
is a lie! You leave yourself out... !

That's all the phantoms can do!
Create a phantom world... !

What freedom is one seeking? Freedom from
wanting life to be other than what it is!

Meditation is at its best
when we step out of the way
and let it happen

What exists in time is nothing but a fleeting shadow
… which-may-be-your-own!

To believe you know the truth is to live in prison

Paths are helpful, perhaps necessary, till
you reach the edge of the cliff!

A false path can be excused
but not a false journey

Knowledge is acquired; Truth is revealed!
... wait your turn

You are always in the Now
There is no other place to be!

Happiness without one moment of unhappiness?
There is nothing like a single-ended stick!

And then... there is the ZEN way of being...
multidimensional - to have no dimensions at all!

Look again!
You may have arrived

How can you be humble, as long as
you know something?

Peace is not a personal achievement; if you are at peace
it's only because, that peace has been given to you

You confuse a description for a prescription
... and that's your misery!

Unless we understand that there is nothing
to understand we understand NOTHING

The disciple wants to know about the unknowable
Out of compassion, the Master speaks about the
unspeakable

It's not your story
It's the story of life

You don't make something out of nothing
No wonder you have no takers whatsoever

It's a matter of definition
What you call zero... I call the infinite!

Have you visited His beauty parlour?
If not, please do
Enter His house and sit in His presence
You are made beautiful, you have no choice

The guy who takes away your religion... will soon
become your new religion!

We know a lot without really knowing anything!

You SIMPLY do not exist! God is ALL there is!
God is EVERYTHING. There cannot be everything
PLUS you

A dubious gift, as it were...
The mind cannot understand What-Is
And What-Is, is-all-there-is!

You haven't got anything from the Master
because you haven't lost anything!

Desirelessness... is the highest form of generosity!

The Master will not even say "'do nothing"
Because he knows you can't even do that!

A "Teaching"... is like a placebo
An illusory antidote for an illusory ailment… Ego

Take your pick...
Either you say everything is acausal
or everything causes everything!

What Is, Is!
Need one say anything more?

If it makes sense I am afraid you have read
the book of life wrong!

You can never have a perfect life
But you can always have a happy one

Let me get this straight... !
I know nothing; but I am not ignorant!

'I am That' means... only 'That' is!
God... is-all-there-is

The mundane is comforting...
... I am truly blessed

The Sage has no message to give
He has only Himself to offer!

Truth is in the discovery
not in the discovered

Why does the evil exist?
Precisely for the same reason that the good does

It's not the darkness itself that stops us from seeing!
… it's the IGNORANCE about the darkness

There is no way out because you are the whole shop!

Illusions ARE meant to be destroyed!
So there is always hope for 'you'

The most important thing that's happening
to your life right now... is-life-itself!

He who sees imprisonment
must be imprisoned himself!

You ask the impossible!
You live in your own world... and yet
ask for a world to live in

I can't cut the long story short
I simply have no story to tell!

Milestones en route to freedom:
I care
I don't care
I don't care even if I do care

You don't get to write the story
You only get to live it!

If you want nothing to be happy, you probably are!

The "final state"... is not the presence
of the belief that you do not exist but
the absence of the belief that you do!

Befooled again... !
My questions were answered; but I wasn't!

Only in surrender... does one know
the real meaning of freedom

And then... one is good
Once there is a knowing... that living itself
is a necessary evil

The moment you think 'I'
you are already a warrior!

The whole point of this drama we call life...
is to realize we're just roles, not the actor

MAYA - a common misunderstanding
shared by all!

You don't go all the way...
If you do, you know you-won't-come-back
Clever you

How is the dreamer concerned
with the contents of the dream?
Ask the awakened! [pun intended]

Floating feet, Heavy mind
One can walk on water and still-be-miserable

There IS a way to accept the world exactly the way
God made it
To be one yourself!!

The absolute is only a concept
The relative is-all-there-is!

If I don't know what I am missing, so be it
It's precisely in trying to have it all that we
lose it all!

In practice… Peace of Mind, can mean only this…
More than wanting to be happy, I don't want
to be unhappy!

When silence... is synonyms with the din... of
the market place, know, that you have arrived!

Rendering spirituality in terms of the every day
I find that all spirituality disappears, the every day
is all that remains

Making a clean break with the past
only means... making a clean break with oneself!

The story will remain the same
but it will not be YOUR story

You confuse a rope for a snake
... and it's not YOUR fault!

God is omnipotent as long as you ask
nothing of Him

You are not the doer! And if you are not the doer
and if you are not in control... what can you do...
except surrender?

Leave it all to destiny, including the 'leaving' of it

Why things are the way they are... ?
No one can know! Not even the SAGE!

Blindingly Obvious
The fish never sees the water. No wonder
we never see God!

You want things to make sense
within your mental frame
Life is too big to draw a box around!

Self-knowledge is actually a misnomer…
In Self-knowledge, there-is-no-place-for-knowledge!

Now, that one is not physically in chains
'bondage' has to be a mere idea

The Sage doesn't get rid of his mind. He just
recognizes it for what it is!
UNDERSTANDING IS ALL

First, there was 'understanding', and then that
which would understand, disappeared

ENLIGHTENMENT means...
outsourcing your life to God!

The not-knowing state puts the world
in its place: Oblivion

The Sage questions our questions with questions
& leaves us with nothing
The 'nothing' that we truly are

Peace is the absence of involvement
in happiness and unhappiness

Enlightenment cannot be achieved; it can
only be accepted

Sage A says "Understanding is all"
"There is nothing to understand" says Sage B
And both are right!

The universe... is not human-centric. It doesn't
operate from an adult human perspective!

Words, try to keep the Truth with a grip that kill it!
What's more they do such a fabulous job!

Seeking HAPPENS... just like everything else...
Did you one day decide... "from tomorrow 9 am
I am going to start seeking enlightenment?"

Real meditation... is accepting life as it happens

Who cares if the phantom is liberated?
Only the other phantoms!

The Jnani sees everything and yet He does not see!
Because He is seeing Himself!

TRUTH if there is one, frees you from itself!

I believe in happiness, only I spell it peace-of-mind!

There is no one who wakes up
when one finally wakes up

Happiness IS enlightenment!
Pursue happiness and get enlightened

You ask 'How to live?', when you are
the living itself!

The world IS a stage … it's just that…
the players have taken the play for real!

Go places you have never been before!
Go INSIDE

How will you find if you are always seeking something?

Beware the signpost!
The best shortcut... is the highway itself!

We see a part & draw the whole... and then
stay blind to the whole forever...

All are called... All are chosen!

... the opposite is true as well! Perhaps more truer!
NO QUESTIONS, NO ANSWERS,
NO ANSWERS... NO QUESTIONS!

You have not as yet questioned the seeking itself!
I am afraid lot of seeking is still to happen

To exist is a lie
The moment you wake-up, you live your lie!

You see everything except what is there!
You-see-nothing!

The way is not really a way...
Where there is a way, there is bound to be
another way

Hell only means believing the stories to be real

I do not know what I intend to do until I do it!
Your guess is as good as mine

FULFILLMENT...
is the end...
of the one...
seeking fulfillment

While reflecting on how to live your life
don't forget to reflect on who lives it!

Kill the ego? But you don't HAVE an ego!
You ARE the ego

The only thing that needs to be treasured is that
which never needs to be treasured

Taking the story to be real
is also part of the story

Heaven and Hell are our own creation
... that doesn't mean we have a choice!

Many wipe the slate clean
It's the rare one who wipes the slate itself!

For a hero to be a hero someone has to
play the villain! What, with duality being
the VERY mechanism of everyday life!

Freedom to a large extent... consists in knowing
what one can't be free from

Teachers… are a varied lot…
Some teach us how to dream
And some… how-to-wake-up!

What do you mean "How?"
Anything can happen!!

Myopia: Thinking of life without thinking of death

If you don't avoid hell… there is no hell anymore!

What God are you seeking... ?
The one who you have made?
or
The one who has made you?

There are no enlightened people, there is only
enlightened living

It's one thing to get disturbed...
Getting disturbed, because you got disturbed
is entirely another

If you say you do not see It, your "not seeing It"
is also It!

It's not a question of seeing things differently
It's seeing things as they are!

Is there something which is not a concept?
ANY answer... WHATSOEVER, will only be
another concept!

The last missing piece of the puzzle
is the puzzler himself!

That's the Paradox!
Only those who flow with life
know what it means to be still

The Sage behaves like a dry leaf in the wind
but then, He knows, that He is the wind too!

Since something happens, it means, it HAD to happen

Desire IS the root cause of sorrow
Only-if-it's-pursued!

I would surely tell you what I am pointing at
had I myself known it!

Delusion... is simply that, which enables
the world... to look the way it does

Your "reality" is a story
A story you tell about What-Is!

To talk about that which can't be talked about!
It's a dirty job, but somebody's got to do it!

All the utterances of a Sage are ultimately silly
and ridiculous!

We are bound... not so much, by the hope of a
better future as by the hope of a better past!

It's ENTIRELY... a matter of grace!
Because it's possible to look, and not SEE

The Master has cut me down to size
The universe is mine!

The good news is that Truth is an open secret
The bad news... is that it-is-not-open-to-all!

PEACE... is simply the realization
that it's impossible for the moment to be otherwise!
And it's not always an easy realization!

I am nothing other than what I am
And I am nothing!

FREEDOM is only the recognition
of one's total powerlessness!

A Sage is what He is! Not what He says!

Misery... is seeking remedy for the ills
that are inseparable from life

The final destination isn't death... !
It's the DEATHLESS

You wouldn't seek God had you not already
found Him!

The mirage remains a mirage even after you know
it to be one
It's just that you stop expecting water from it

You look SOLELY through the eyes of time, and then
cry foul that the timeless eludes you!

The Sage is that person who is no person
He is every person

The so-called seeker will not go to a REAL Sage
A real Sage won't tell him, what he wants to hear

While fighting you have to be careful not to destroy
the thing that you are fighting for!

Explain you can...
But you will never be able to explain your explanation!

Do ghosts exist? If God can create embodied entities
what stops Him from creating disembodied entities?

In DEEP SLEEP... we are all enlightened!

Making something out of Nothing... !
God did exactly that when He created the world!

A person is more of a story than a fact
No wonder... we have story-tellers, one TOO MANY
Story-busters... HARDLY any

The phantom has no choice but feed
on-other-phantoms

The only absolute knowledge or understanding...
is that which cannot be spoken, and which cannot
even-be-known!

We don't exist to serve reality
...we exist... to serve the illusion

You don't have to like every single character
... to enjoy the movie!

One who feels free to be bound
is a great deal less bound

Happiness is not found. It is noticed

All you have got to show for a lifetime of seeking
is just this - an ostentatious display of yardsticks
meant to measure the immeasurable!

There are no prerequisites for waking up
other than being asleep

MAN, PRETENDING TO BE GOD
is one BIG BIG joke! Because, ALL he truly is, is
GOD, PRETENDING TO BE MAN!

We are NOT TWO. You are ANOTHER me
A duet of One, so to speak

When that, which would accept is no longer present
the acceptance is total!

The Sage is one who demystifies...
He is never the one who mystifies

You may not like the way you are made
You just have to accept it

To have it all, one has to not only have it all
but know as well that one has it all!

Concept of God, is useful, in removing the concept
of the individual

ZEN is like reading a detective story with the
last page missing… ! It REMAINS a mystery

It is good to become enlightened
Just don't take it personally!

Living ITSELF is all the meditation necessary

To see that things aren't, is to see things
as they are!

Does the sun see darkness?
The Jnani sees no difference between the saint
and the sinner!

Was Buddha someone else?
Was He not yourself?

One can't be friends with the part...
One can only be friends with the whole

Trying to find the absolute
in the realm of the relative
is what spiritual seeking is all about

Before finding, if heaven and hell are for real
find out, if there is "someone" to go there

MAYA... simply means, being under the spell
of God's DIVINE-HYPNOSIS... and nobody
but ONLY He, who has induced the hypnosis
can remove it

Why is the leaf green?
The leaf is green because it's green
is as good an answer as any

And once you catch sight of Him...
Masked! Unmasked! You will see only Him, all around
again & again & again!

What does it matter? Saying that the ghost exists
only in the mind doesn't make it any less a ghost!

He... who created the world will look after it
Let God do His job!

There are but two ways of seeing...
Arjuna's way - from which problems never cease!
Krishna's way - from which problems never arise!

SUFFERING is best defined, as the gap, between
how things ARE... and how things should BE

I sometimes wonder... in self-deception
who deceives whom?

A monk asked, "Where do the stars come from?"
The master said, "Where did the question come from?"

You have answers for everything
You have reasons for everything
You have explanations just for everything!
Clearly you like the idea of playing God

It is I that exists in all that exists!

To the truly enlightened, nothing is sacred
or perhaps everything is!

You have always found... what you truly desire
when you have no desire

It's simple!
All you have to do... is find a path
where journeying is ITSELF the biggest obstacle
in reaching the destination

You don't have independent power
because-you-are-not-independent!

Poetic allusions... to reality
What we call scriptures are just that!

That which needs to know itself is always the ego
The real... can only be itself!

The cast isn't happy. But the movie
is-already-in-the-can!

Once you realize that a belief is only a belief
and just that, the question of getting rid of it
doesn't-arise-at-all!

Empty handed I went to the master
Empty handed I returned... What luck!

You are not in bondage
You... ARE the bondage

There is no agony... like the agony
of trying to grasp something...
which can only come to you of itself!

You are but a robot!
And a robot cannot be happy or unhappy

Where... the puppeteer is-himself-a-puppet... !
No puppet-show... like the puppet-show of life

You don't have to go back the way you came
You-never-left-home!

The creator… is in the creation
You separate the creator from the creation
and look-for-him!

To become that, what-you-cannot-not-be
no master can help you

You are, what you are in deep sleep
Every morning you wake up in someone else

Advice for the spiritually "advanced"
While you're busy getting your questions answered
don't forget to get your answers questioned!

Understand you will... but not as long as
you want to make it "your" understanding

The realization is not only that one is unreal
but that at the same time one is real!

All knowledge is ignorance... !
Every time you say "I don't know"... know
that you are spot-on!

It's not that one is happy in deep sleep, but rather
there is no one to be happy or unhappy

Where nothing is, nothing can be missing...

I am content to have my wordless treasure
Who cares who has the last word!

The Master wears no mask, so yours can fall

Awakening... is a droplet in the ocean... coming
to understand that what it truly is...is the ocean
Deliverance is the complete dissolution of the droplet
that would have this understanding!

All there is, is consciousness! Period
... rest ALL... is merely gift-of-the-gab

Mahesh Hangal, ever since he can remember considers himself a 'professional spiritual seeker'. His search for 'the peace that surpasseth all understanding' took him to Osho, U G krishnamurti & many many others. He is extremely well read. He is more than conversant with Zen, Tao, Advaita and other spiritual stuff. He has dabbled in reiki, trancedental meditation, E.F.T & other self-help techniques/ therapies/meditations. His seeking finally ended when he met the advaitic sage Shri Ramesh Balsekar. Reading Wayne Liquorman [disciple of Ramesh Balsekar & an advaitic sage himself] further grounded him in the 'understanding'.

Mahesh has also published a book of Urdu/Hindi ghazals titled 'Lo fir hai saamne deewar koi'. He ran a book library for over thirty four years. He was an event organizer as well, specializing in... Indian classical music events. Mahesh happens to be the grandson of the renowned Indian classical vocalist Dr. Gangubai Hangal. He is presently a mutual fund distributor.

He is a bachelor and resides in Hubli, Karnataka, India. When he was asked to tell something more about himself he flippantly quoted a musing of his "Apart from the story of the world, I have no story of my own".

Email. maheshhangal@yahoo.com
Cell. +91 95389 34989

(Graffiti is a revised and updated version of my earlier book titled 'Scribblings')